Assumptions Of Heart

(Presenting Poetries)

by

Anjali Shah

Assumptions Of Heart
(Presenting Poetries)

by Anjali Shah

ISBN: 978-93-62207-02-9

Published by

DOUBLE 9 BOOKS
2/13-B, Ansari Road
Daryaganj, New Delhi – 110002
info@double9books.com
www.double9books.com
Tel. 011-40042856

ABOUT THE AUTHOR

I am Anjali Jagdish kumar Shah has written the book "Assumptions Of Heart". I am currently a student pursuing Bachelor Of Ayurvedic Medicine And Surgery from K.J. Institute Of Ayurveda, Savli, Vadodara. I had completed my schooling as a science student from Smt. M.M.Mehta English Medium School, Palanpur. Along with that I always had a thought of studying literature and so I do prefer reading certain Poetries and Novels; and with that; I started writing poetry on different experiences of mine , emotions and yeah certainly imaginations too. So this being my very first book, it is really connected to me with all my heart and feelings underneath. Hoping the reader can relate with the poetries that I had written.

CONTENTS

11. Highly Divine

12. Heath Being Prime

13. Over Dramatic

1.
He ♡ & The Story

Wanna Date You

Your fierce eyes
And your small small lies
Your mesmerizing talks
Comes to my heart and knocks

With the hot headed jaw
I swear you look so sharp as if a Raw ….
Wanna pull your cheeks and bite it slightly
Don't blush too much….take it lightly

Want your dreamy lips to utter that words
But sometimes you seem as if a duffer nerd
I being sugar, sweet and cute
Wondering mainly ….why you are on mute?

Sometimes I feel, I wanna date you….
But your 6 feet height that's the reason I do hate you
Dear Tom Cruise Twin
Wanna snatch your heart and win

Don't you think, You should be mine
Ask me for a date if it is fine
Yes, I probably make wait you
But deep inside I Wanna Date You…

~ *Anjali Shah*

Describing Him ❣️□

He is twilight....
In my darkest nights....
My aggressive violence,
And his peaceful silence....
Speaks a lot, And his sorry makes everything sort.......

His eyes being thunder striking.....
And his arms around me,
Being divine vibing
Loving and Intense is he,

He is sensitive as if a kiddo....
But his innocence with me is never at veto .....
Being not so descent.....
Holding my hands and a deep kiss on my lips that's his recent.....

As mentioned earlier....
Being unknown he was still familiar......
How to tell you ! How is he!
Only my eyes does know .....
His name is inscribed within me....

I love him till the eternity.....
And his love for me is infinity......

~ *Anjali Shah*

You Are The Reason....!

I used to weep alone
But nowadays there is Invisible shoulder bone....
On which my head can rest and rely
And that too for me it never deny....

The way moon spreads a bit light in darkness...
You are my heart , before that was heartless....
Though I am a tiny divine
But you are charming monstrous of mine....

With the dreams of risky tipsy night to climbing Alps
Ain't walking isolated, together taking trivial steps....
The desperately holded hands
Having butterscotch feelings inside that never want to have ends....

Away from the future parting worries....
Want to be with you, without no limits and no boundaries....
The heart beats faster and announces my living life:
You Are The Reason with that I am still Alive !

~ Anjali Shah

Face Time

With lots of butterflies chuckling inside
Face Time we both tried
The man was all in black
And I had messy track
Being shy with no filters the face was upfront
And my roomies muddling, need to have exeunt
The awkward blushes
And his observation all over it rushes
No words were uttering
" Your eyes is so pretty " , that was his buttering.
Not so smooth but it was cute
We ended our face time that was majorly on mute!

~ *Anjali Shah*

Thousands Miles Away From You

Thousands miles away from you
Learning to survive without you
No messages, No calls….
And tears from eyes falls

Distance increasing day by day
Now it seems, there is no way
Missing you a lot
But bounded by sad strain thought

Do I still feel?
This question never gets heal
A admiring text away from Thousands miles
And soon my face smiles. 😊
Thousands Miles Away From You

~Anjali Shah

My Moonshadow

Hey My Moonshadow !
Your soul in darkness, for me it's a peaceful shallow....
Have your delighted arms around my curves....
And that cuddling night vibes around my nerves....
The sky being black and tragic....
Spread your deep voice whisper magic.....
Hey My Moonshadow!

~ Anjali Shah

Good Night

The Vibes That Invade Between
The Talks That Shared Through A Small Screen...

A Reality Still Seems A Reel Dream,
And Prayed For Forever Esteem

New Day Tomorrow With The New Light,
Close Your Eyes And Have A Good Night....

~ Anjali Shah

I just can't believe

Baby, I just can't believe
You the world, I dreamt

From the uphill sky to down
You the reason of my Crown
I just love to be with you
Holding your with you hands (and) cuddling too Yeah

Holding your hands (and) cuddling too

And Baby , I just can't believe
You the world, I dreamt

Your smile is my breathe
And the life to sustain with
Getting crazy with your talks
Leaving all the crowded flocks...

And Baby, I just can't believe
You the world, I dream*t*...

~ Anjali Shah

Lost In You

A new request, I found out
Accepted it, Thinking no back out
"Unknowns but still were known...
Almost two years, together we grown

Deep shallow voice, listening to it without a noise
Felt all the weathers of mature man
To the childish chattering can

The journey was of two individual people
Soon their souls were rippled
"Sugar' wasn't just a name but a feeling
And Duffer' was a nerd being introvert who was revealing....

Only their eyes know,
The painful rain of highs and low....
No grudges but still lots of complains
Without any explanation the parting explains

Those intense eyes, Those cute talks, Those smiling cheeks
Uff..... Sorry ! No clicks.
That was you;

Somewhere still "Lost In You"

~ *Anjali Shah*

That's It !

27th July 2022

11:53 pm (Text)

He :- That's it then..... 1 year 6 months and 16 days

Counts for 562 days and around 13,440 hours

She :- Is it actually that's it ?

And they both still being together smiles on the above texts ♡

2.
Cynical Relationship (Dark side Of A Relation)

Untold

Darksoul, it But what was a dark night for you
But what can I do?
If my heart beats for you
I know,
We ain 't sailing in the same boat
The way you do love me, I don't.
Our pathways are different
And those feelings ain't liberal
"Should we leave each other ?"
And having this question….. My heart aches
Why this love differences takes place ?
Emotions are still left untold

More things are still left in other chapter to unfold

~ *Anjali Shah*

I Thought....!

I thought I am always running in your brain....
I thought I should always stick by you.....
I thought I might be your priority....
I thought I should never pretend fake towards you....
I thought I and you , we are made for each other.....
I thought I love u And u too love me....
But soon
I realised it was all just ; I thought...!

~ Anjali Shah

Things Does Change!

When situation was busy
We still had time!
Now when I am free and so does he
Yet there's no hour to be with!
And so things does change.....
From the range of friendship to range of love
From the range of unknown to range of know....
And then completely back to be strangers
Things does change!

~ Anjali Shah

Nightmare Of Broken Dream?

Still it's a illusion

He Confronted

He Talked

He Liked

He Loved

He Cared

He Missed

He Waited

He Missed Me Again

He Loved Me More

And suddenly He didn't Care Anymore

He Cheated On !
Once, Twice, Thrice and so on…

It was all about him!
Where was I in this all?
And I found myself at the point where
I was
believing him blindly and loving him immensely

This All Being A Nightmare Or Broken Dream..
When I opened my eyes there was nothing ….
Still I found myself being hurt…..
I found myself in deep sentiments and illusion…

~ Anjali Shah

Someone And Somewhere

I don't know why nowadays things for me are just

Disturbance

Disappearance

Disappointments

Distractions

Depression

Anxiety

Fear

And

Somewhere maybe I lost you .....!

Hey, Are You Still There ?!

Or your beloved heart beats for someone and somewhere....!

~ Anjali Shah

Moonshadow

I do have that worst memories scars!
Will Share them to Moonshadow in night stars… .
And she said this to herself ;

And after listening he soon asked himself;
Leave my hands and let me fall .....

But he got hurt after all!

~ Anjali Shah

Falling in Love .....

Falling in Love is okay
Driving crazy for someone is also ok....
Crying over the same person again and again....
Is that okay ?!
When you know there won't be any solution to it...!
Still a person enters to the vicious cycle again and again

To be honest
In search of serenity
Just found a way of leaving everyone....
And Staying All Alone

~ *Anjali Shah*

I Dressed The Same

I dressed the same… The way I planned for
Had carried revealing dress the way u like…
Blushing face was expected
But a dull sober chid was found….

Tears were rolling down…
Though the busy crowd was around….
With the day passed… Hurting Vibes were prone….
Holded hands were somewhere still alone…

Thoughts of cute clicks together…
It was sham smile rather….
A long waiting vibes…
Provides pull of pieces for life…

~ *Anjali Shah*

Lie Rattles....

Again there were teary eyes... Still I was able to hide....

Ain't alone and was between the crowd .... Still ! My bad , I did abide...

Again was awake and no sleep to rely...

I feel self respect is almost ended but I do deny...

Thoughts in brain battles...

And all over lie rattles....

~ Anjali Shah

Tired Of His Fake words...

Tired Of His Fake words
Left my obligations and opened his hands' cuffs....
Let him explore and be friendly free
I can't take those lies cloudy breeze....

Those special things he did was hardly mine....
Knew it before but being shut kept it fine...
My personal life is all publicated...
But being shut diplomatically he dated....

Maybe I am dumb forever...
Shh ! Relationship truth he wouldn't say it ever...
Don't know who will regret either me or him...
To be honest... Hoping he should never... !

A parted by the closest one....
As my past says ; Playing The Victim For Fun !
~ Anjali Shah

It's All Burning From Inside

It's all burning from inside....

The man who is my a lot....
His best half always struggled for his love and fought...
Want to escape from all this miseries....
And want to fly with that cool wind breeze

Behaving as if immature and childish kid....
And no one can notice that sobbing chide...
Difficult sustenance but with all strength she tried.....
Trust Me! It's all burning from inside....

Letting yourself out can cause worst ramifications.....
Dying for the pride but still in that ego – expectations.....
Heaps of hate yet with love it's tied.....
Yes, it's all burning from inside....

~ Anjali Shah

Hey, I am fallen for you indeed

I don't wanna be so rude
But I am getting such nowadays
I know it's ruining my relation
With you;
that hurts you got,
Are not easy to be carried away…

Hey, I am guess fallen for you indeed
But I guess it's turned to my need

That long distance sucks
ALL the frustration is getting on my nerves
I wanted my love to last for long
But , I hardly know to whom my heart belongs ….

It's not mine anymore and it's not even yours…
Just lost in the past pain and deep thoughts…

Hey , I am still fallen for you indeed
But I guess it's turned to my need

~ Anjali Shah

Retrieve

I didn't cry lost single tear this time,
And the last goodbye wasn't mine....
Though My mistake but still the world was blamed ....
Heart differences are always at the aim...

"I don't fucking were his care whom you're texting ",
Were his exact words...
Just close your eyes and keep on resting
Whispered my past burns......

Started with the hope of healing ,
Ended with the piece of pain feeling ;
One more unseen damage , Hence Retrieve...

~ Anjali Shah

Leftover

I just wanna be free bird
Bonded in love we were
Hopes twined out to hell
Oh gosh! Hauntingly we fell

Promises turned out toxic
Head with thoughts, "Loss sick"!
Leftover of why and if !
With smile we do weep

Still in false seeming affection
Burning fire pain sensation
Broken trust, with feel and lust
Caring vibes still sustain
Shh! Hide it with ignorance curtain...

~ Anjali Shah

Destroyer

You were the ray that shine
Holding your hands & I will be fine
On the seventh cloud but felt it nine
And Hey Mr. Are you mine?

Shattered heart pieces
And made it whole
You became my destiny
And the goal
Let's just love
And there came a U turn curve
Pretty more girls around, that wasn't fine
Dropped down from the seventh & the nine…

You were that 'Destroyer' that came to lie…
I was dumb that I called you my!

~ Anjali Shah

Good Bye!

It was all started mesmerising
And soon it ended depressing
Things were going in perfect raft....
And now the old texts are just saved in draft...

Closeness was deeply awaited ....
But soon in few years it faded.....
Promise of forever to be spent together....
Suddenly changed as if a weather.....

Things are going bloody hell
Oops ! Sorry I can't tell...
Now this reasons tell are given
And good vibes are somewhere driven......

Eyes waiting to be with ....
This thought doesn't allow me to breathe.....
Things started with a Hi!
And it came to the point to say Good Bye!
~ *Anjali Shah*

3.
COMICAL TIME 🤭

Does All Poets Are Broken?

I asked him to suggest me something to write…..

He replied, "Broken heart gives a deep down poetry…!"

And soon;

As he loved me and wanted me to be good poet,

He Broke my Heart …..

Meanwhile me being still in illusion,
"Aww… he did this as he really loves me "
hehe… Lol
(Just being the joke of the day)

~ Anjali Shah

Ain't Jesting But That Several Freakish First Call !

Though I being a Extrovert
Having talks in me as if a never ending desert……

That day I went disquieted…..
And no talks in me were enlightened……

He made a phone call and I received…..
And at the second moment the silence was perceived……

Not me, Not even him, None uttering a single word out……
Inside me and him, may be there was a shyness sprout…..

After waiting for a while to speak up, the call was cut…..
Deep in, I did know he is a Duffer nut….

Again the call was made…..
And from both the sides hi-hello held…..
Arrived the stillness….
And their blushing face were witness…..

Having little compassion on his nerves…..
Inner me, I know he loves…..
Oops And the call was end….
The last trial of the day was having freakish tend…..
What a Divine topic he started on
Being sarcastic above, the topic was Study Schedule' and he had a tutor tone…..

Had a continuous conversation for long 3 minutes…..
"Well, Physics is hard, let's start with Biology units….!
Being notorious I asked, This is what we are going to talk?
And he being shy, the call came to ending mock….

Ain't Jesting But That Several Freakish First Call
Along with his innocence, made me Fall…..

For him 🤭

~ Anjali Shah

Idiotic Mock !

Yesterday was so awkward!
His crazy childhood friend, (she)
Texted me from his Instagram I'd
I thought that was he !
Starting held with normal lock talk key....
Sudden the sincere boy went stud,
How ? I don't know but still I felt ......
All those blonde laughter talk was all over left...

This morning brought me in the shock
Got to know that was her.... And I had idiotic mock
Previous night the shared me her click,
Pretending as if him ; she asked should I have hook up blink
And I being dumb suggested
She looks living makeup shop and thank god she didn't busted....

She was hot,
Though I commented in my second thought....

Today when I got to know the reality
I got this all clarity
But Thank god my friend from Pak
Though yesterday night I got in dark
Is that sincere man who does poetry !

~ *Anjali Shah*

The Rainy Day ♡

Planning was done to go out and chill...
And the sky had no cloudy feel...
Had opened silky hair...
Dressed in comfy trousers wear...

My mate along with me was excited ...
Hardly any crowd were invited...
Till the point we reach to cafe....
The clear sky was wet being astray...

Went wet like a wet cat...
And had food like a mad rat..
Though I took bath in the morning ...
But rain wet look was adorning...

Two partners but they were shut...
The way was long but seems short cut..
Still confused about enjoying ...
Maybe somewhere raindrops were annoying..

Was way back to hostel and saw a watery pit..
Jumped like a little kid but the fun was lit..
Made my look go dirty...
Clothes went whole muddy....
Was just like a peppa pig...

Flaunted in fun like a historian wigg... 🤭

Ahh ! My favourite rainy day...

Next day on bed due to fever it made me stay... 👉👈

~ Anjali Shah

Loop Hole...

Ain't having anything to write....
Well, He was white....
With the things does change!
I had a long idiotic mock range .....
Twist and turns come to the point,
Of being alone and alone (Reprise)....
Hiding myself behind the fake lies
Hehe.... Let's have a check on safety caution,
Does all poets are broken?
Is still the question...
Poetry made me know, Wondering soul,
Here I completed the poetry ' Loop Hole...'
(of my own poems titles)

~ Anjali Shah

Tale of Mr. Charming

In such fairy tale stories,
I wasn't princess of glories....
And Mr. Charming wasn't that brave,
So before it begins, the tale was end to grave......

With no flock myths ,
There was a devil with scythe....
And the love thread was cut,
As it was just fly and flirt...
Never mind it didn't hurt!

At the climax, Mr. Charming was single sole....
And so I was single left unattached, lol
!

~ Anjali Shah

4.
SAD STRAIN 😟

Alone

"Alone - Alone" A voice from heart came along,
Stone threw to is was heard having pain since long…

Uphill the sky,
Each and Everyday sunken by the lie ….
Round and round talks around,
Without external injury till wound….

Can't evoke the sad strain,
And can't deny the eyes filled with awful rain…
Internal peace lying at the ease,
Broken myself into millions of piece….

"Alone - Alone", A voice from heart came along,
Stone threw to it was heard having pain since long....

~ *Anjali Shah*

Toxicity

Toxicity is at the stake
Still insanity is my first take
Now, worthy days are there
Want to step up but how do I dare?

Everyone wants to claim
And failure comes to blame
Not so working hard
And question mark on the career card

I want to do this but you have to do that
No one cares about two opposing fact
Soon the failure will arrive
And blame and sadness will get alive

Fucking by the world around ....
Oops ! You are Responsible , this sound
Deep pain and fierce beneath...
Want my dreams to be mine and Breathe!

~ Anjali Shah

Bounded Boundaries

Hating myself at the times
And being guilty for not so worthy crimes
Freedom snatched, Limits are bounded,
Inside me, I am wounded

A big mistake of my life,
Is now cutting me with the knife....
I being fed up of clearing the doubts,
And pretending fake just like the crowd

With the wind blowing high,
Take me away to touch the sky....
Give me little wings of birds to fly,
Away from the dignity and no tears to cry.....

With the brain having no worries,
Take me away from the boundaries....

~Anjali Shah

Alone (Reprise)

Inside somewhere the internal voice screams, ' You are Alone',

Outside, eyes watching surrounded by too many vocalize tone…

"I'm there for you", people says having wonderful attire,

Whenever need arrives, it feels as if it was just a satire..

"Alone-Alone" a voice from heart came along,

Stone threw to it, was heard having pain since long…

~ *Anjali Shah*

At the edge of life

At the edge of life,
Stabbed and slammed by the knife....
Getting low, Getting down,
Losing self gifted Crown...

Ten more reasons I found,
They all looked profound
Having heart ache,
Called them as mine' but snake!

One more driven U-turn ,
Let me move out and run ......
Stop! That's what I want to say,
To the Relations made of clay....

At the edge of life .....
Stabbed and Slammed by the knife!

~ *Anjali Shah*

5.
CRUSH – I ADORE HIM♡

Correspondence with Maturity ♡

I don't know exactly from where to start...
My Ideal ! And Lots of things I want to draft...
Short and Cute but still as if a storm...
Hardly I saw him in swarm ....

The sweetest smile that he passes of...
My class girls having fondling crush drops...
Me being a secret observer....
Noticed his eyes with patience cover...

Yes a quiet authentic soul for me...
But I found a bond as if friendly free...
I am always into ramifications...
He helping me out with simplifications..

I learned to move on ...
Even his story went wrong...
Some similarities are the reason...
Such as exploring and enjoying seasons...

His long fluffy hair...
And such descent nature is rare....
That profile pic I still do recall....
Maybe a reason that I had a great fall...

From beard to moustache...
I being in notorious stage...
Crowd discussed why did he trim so sudden...
Sarcasm ! Maybe that was his girlfriend's burden...

I being Horrid Henry Of His life....
Felt good every time when I had talking vibe....
Lots of things I had shared...
And he secretly cared...

It's the cutest correspondence with maturity that I found....
Ideal forever and that's profound... ♡

~ Anjali Shah

Wavy Hairs

Wavy hairs and sparkled smile...
Took me to open eyes dream for a while...
Can I hold your veiny hands?
But there will be miserable ends...

Your Flirtatious Replies...
I knew but ignored it wise....
Was bounded though...
Still bounded flow....

It won't be forever I guess...
And my sensitive feelings won't be at rest...
You want it flirt and fly !
And I will want you to be my....

Pain in eyes and you were about to hug...
But limitations are all stuck...
Will let you know before we apart...
The unfolded relief, would be my part !

~ *Anjali Shah*

Q/A sessions

And the day was as usual....
Though informed not to dress casual...
Not so tough job but it was confined voce...
And to be honest there we do get our restricted dose...

For me it seemed different....
Those vibes on my nerves still passing efferent...
My Eyes taker ; was dressed in green phthalo…
Me being novice was trying talent of willo....

The Grin On his face....
Makes me blank all with the ace...
The questions just being formality...
Answered them wrong and away from reality....

Was smiling and had redden cheeks...
And his denomination towards the trippy trick ...
Happiness and a together trip is a synonym..
New philosophical truth being our antonym....

His eyes gives me escaping from worries vibes...
And my brain rhyming pleasant scribes....

~ Anjali Shah

TRUST KNOT ♡

Started with a scary Saturday.....
Too many lies and a risky stay....
Surrounded by thoughts....
But had a tight trust knot....

A hug that was long awaited....
And all nervousness was fainted....
My first and somewhere his first time too....
His head on her laps and had she had no clue...

She Scrolled his phone from up to down....
And his hands were around....
Couple dance for couple of times....
That contained a different vibes....

Was comfy for sure....
And his cuteness on refusal was to adore....
A kiss on forehead
And a tight hug like a ted...
This was all according to the plan.....

~ *Anjali Shah*

A Nostalgic Night ♡

The moon was elated ,
And doze in eyes was painted....
His head near her heart ;
And No gap to apart....

Soon, Locked by heart raising cuddle ;
And shyness was about to shuttle...

Lips smoothing touches,
Soft Kisses and blushes,
Arms around the curves,
Mesmerizing feeling all over the nerves....

Sleepy eyes being awake...
Hint of lips was sure to make,
Her hands on his neck,
Into tasting him was next....
Feet meddling with ;
Hands holded and deep breathe...

Yes ! She was In love somewhere...
But at the end was handle with care....
Her Denial made him stay away
Close but still there's no way....

From Sin Of Never....
For him changed it to ever....
Didn't feel it wrong...
And wanted to be with along....

Soon eyes were closed….
And the moment was froze…
Darkness turned bright ....
Nostalgic Night… ♡

~ Anjali Shah

Mysterious 👀

Yes My Brain Got Diverted For A While !
Stuck by the past memories and asked for a Retrial...
Little my eyes did weep
And then after had a good sleep...
Woke up with the thought in mind ;
The reality might be hurtful to unwind.....
Again didn't want the lately parting raft :
And so did expunge the sent draft...
Those Evocations are really precious...
Let it be certainly Mysterious !

~ Anjali Shah

(Crush Never Stays For Long)

6.

SHE

Secrets Inside

There are millions of laughs,
Hiding millions of tears....

Deep in eyes,
There are secrets inside.....

Making world to believe,
There's no internal relief....

Fake smile, Fake glowing face ,
Hiding pain in heart's ace.....

Need a band of twilight,
To make the mood delight....

There are millions of laughs,
Hiding millions of tears....
Deep in eyes,
There are Secrets Inside...

~ *Anjali Shah*

I found myself Hating her millions of times!

A small created mess ,
And that drastically changes into a clash
Her words makes me feel, ' I am a trash! '
And so I found myself Hating her millions.....
But soon without her sorrow climbs.....
Her love for me is as if sour limes,
Sometimes divine , sometimes reason of Teary vibes....

~ Anjali Shah

Puzzle Has Been Solved Zero Times

Played with the feelings a lot
Lastly the victim card ; and No one has caught
Not being guilty then why crying for own lies ?
And this puzzle has been solved zero times!

Laughing, Enhancing with the criminals flock
Will smash oneself And hardly someone mock
One needed countdown to realise but why do I realize ?
And this puzzle has been solved zero !

Sharp view site that makes people fallen and hypnotise
Oh gosh ! Just talking about wondering eyes
Playing games being wise then why pain is hidden in those pretty eyes ?
And This puzzle has been Solved zero times!

"Broken One?' And the answer came "Nah!"
Trust Issues? " And the sound was "Han!"
Own ones tried her to molest and she can't even protest
But still was said ; it was hard-core test

Unrevealed Stories revealed in rhymes
But , Yet, Still Puzzle has been solved zero times!

~ Anjali Shah

Disappeared

She was there somewhere,
Like a insane innocent flower
She A bit crazy... A bit smartly whizzy......

Things were in perfect raft....
And no messages will be saved in draft .....

Brownie being a console mate
And hardly someone hate....
In the search of new life ......
She lost the previous one.....

Some pages were burnt......
But feelings still unburnt....
Those eyes were in tears .....
And inside, lots of fears....

Poetry left incomplete....
As she disappeared in that temper heat...

~ *Anjali Shah*

Black Hole 👀

A loop with no escape....
Seems dangerous and leads to mental death....
Images pretty like Town Cap....
Be with me ! Common Gesture Of Faith...

Imperfections makes a person perfect...
Well but it seems as a threat...
Secrets are deep and dark...
Emotions being thundering spark...

One ,Two and It's Three....
Yet me wants to be with boundaries free...
One does cry for me....
Scary affection I do have with three...
Second, Runs in my mind and heart , "We!"

A false trust hole and truth is black...
A loop with no escape…

~ Anjali Shah

A piece to withstand

A piece to withstand their moods…
A piece to cherish their all goods….

A piece to expel their depressive suffer….
A piece to behold their buffers….

Left outs of their pasts….
Over me, All it is casts…

No friends that's what my instant reaction place it takes….
Truthful and miserably even me fakes….

~ Anjali Shah

U ain't that fragile !

Dark Ruinous Nights

Days With No Lights

Misbehaviour of someone

Alone ! Left by loved one

Umm… Molestation and many more attacks

Mentally over view mainly many lacks

U are wrong ! If u re feminine…

Girly Tantrums , And he went beneath the line…

That's how people judged !

And they called characterless clutch …

Having male friends is obsession ,

I think they never passed victim lessons

Well well well
Closing eyes for a while
"Girl u ain't that fragile",
That's what my heart says
Handle it all with the smile that stays…!

~ Anjali Shah

7.
BUDDY 🤝

Hot Topic 🤭

Things went so weird...
To be honest lots of things were cleared....
I don't know where to stop...
And what things to abort....

Being shut having ache in throat...
Rather than flowing, words are clot....
A bond to survive....
Comes to the point of buffer and retrieve...

Starving for your attention...
That day those stares were having passion...
Yes you are still important...
Attachment and friendship potent...

From that shyness to holder...
Created Gujarati words separate folder...
Thanks for making me learn a lot...
And for those smiles that you brought...

Maybe Focus Forever....
Getting Apart , Nah ! Never...
For those who calls you were time pass...
Sorry people , I do friendship with sensitive class...

Hopeless but still hopeful...

Maybe hot topics that still rule... 🤞🤭♡

~ Anjali Shah

Actin And Myosin

Being on back bench
Smashing each other's clench...
Undertaking Cold War revenge,
The science lecture seems class of French... !

Being actin and he is myosin
Forming thick myofilament bond scene....
Played thumb smash hand game...
Everyone noticing the shameless shame...

Head was down and hairs were pulled...
Answered with a smash and yes I ruled !

~ *Anjali Shah*

Smiles

Their smiles is still affectionate virtue....
For me, will care and respect is forever clue...
A small things occurs to them...
And I feel tensed lame....

Was together but still too many gathers.....
Separate , Apart is just words as flowing feathers....
Mischievous prank calls and Saturday Night...
With those dares, laughing faces were Bright...

One was having spectacles, cute heroine of our teasing kind of stories...
Second being her roomie though had no worries....
Third was laughing chattering box during every class....
The fourth one was queen of hairy mass...

Yes five were shinning but still those 4 shines...
Lost and Untold yet mines....
Floor was noisy and now there's silence..
But underground news are intense...

Eyes does have endearment feel...
Though with grudges, maybe deep beneath I am yours still.... ♡

~ Anjali Shah

Few Lines Of Her

With uncertainty I met her
Same batch still had a differ
Accounted her slowly steadily while going for daily dinner
With no time , she became my together crime sinner
Long Walks ;
Tremendous Gossip Talks…
Laughing and chuckling together
And her fruit salad choosing over anything is better….
From twinning the garba dresses,
Affection she possess….
She being a divine chubby friend ,
Always on double meaning trend 😂

~ Anjali Shah

8.
Pen Friend 🖋️👨💻

Wondering Soul

I met a wondering soul….
For me, He being a mysterious black hole......
Deep inside I wanted to enter more....
But as you know, unknowns are harm to explore.......

Soon , I felt him as if a serious emotion.....
And his face seems to me , Innocent Ocean….
With that black suit gentleman look….
He become confidential character of my book

Playful smile like a child......
But I do doubt, lots of sentiments he does hide….
No crush.... No girlfriend.... he had described…
Well, High Tides in his heart is personified....

He appears busy insect keeping beetle…
Romance -Drama Atonement is his cup of movie kettle….
Philosophy at the stake …m.
For him Creativeness is the love lake.....

I felt him as it a inspirational genre.....
I am as if his life's Henry…
Trying to define the cherish divine.......
I hope after this all…You are fine!

~ Anjali Shah

Crush of famous glory

I got to know his high school story…
Between the books, He was crush of famous glory….
Not so interested in that girl......
He made his separate messy world… .

Well, he is nerd being mysterious man…..
I ain't rating you but still would say you are ten on ten…

~ Anjali Shah

He was in white

Bored in the house beneath
Taking negative things as if a true myth
And soon he arrived
And my musing despised

Umm.... In the group, he was in white
Glowing star in that descent light...

~ Anjali Shah

Hehe!

Too serious for me
(And)
I am the one who does... hehe...
He ain't a early bird...
And his hair, the curly world...

He said, He laughed
In the photograph he made me see...
Me searching with glasses on Eyes
Trying to make the sincere, the chuckling hypnotise...

~ Anjali Shah

(Please smile)

Can I have you in my arms?

Now to this creative world
Lost in thoughts and what I suffer
Planning to have a together supper
Still a learner, And mistakes are all upper

Will love the most if you will teach me
Soon entering into the family so called ' We '
Poetry seems to be red as if a marble
Tried to be little smart.... I hope I am humble

In love with the way you write
I hope I will be able to match your creativity's height
Last thing I want to ask ,

Can I have you in my arms?
A Tight hug with all the warms......

~ Anjali Shah

9.
Short Poems

No one Cares

People are going to laugh on your miseries.....
But still they will pretend to be sad for you...
No one cares to be honest…

The person who cares about ,
Is only you yourself......!

(Lost)

~ Anjali Shah

! Safety Caution!

Falling isn't in your hands ;
But
Saving yourself from a great fall,
Is still somewhere in your hands.....!

~ Anjali Shah

Discard

Long distance is always hard….
'Can't take it more! ': he said;
And left me as a discard....

~ Anjali Shah

Involved

Study factors but my brain making arts
Sleepy most of the time, still crafting crafts
Important lectures I Want to be out & bunk
Mind roaming ; climbing thoughts on trunk…

May be brain building mystery unsolved
Being notorious, yes I am involved…

~ Anjali Shah

Reasons....

When A Person Lose Interest In You
He Stops Noticing You
Behaves Rude and Defensive
Replies Late
And Hides
Reasons Are At The Top
👀

~ Anjali Shah

Nightmares

Those Nightmares That I Suffered Before Being With You....
I was still okay
But after being with you
The Nightmares I faced…
That Broke me!

~ Anjali Shah

Just Ignore The Back Flocks ! 

If people talks bluffs
Let them fall to that extent...
U shouldn't care!
Have your next move and let them stare…

Just ignore the back flocks !
And Your lively smile rocks…

~ Anjali Shah

Why So Tough!

Around the crowd...
Laughing and being aloud...
And sometimes all alone I am crowned....
Deep inside desperately in delusion drowned....

All the examinations passing out....
But the fact is want to fly out....

~ Anjali Shah

10.
SELF MOTIVATING □

You Messed With Wrong!

I tried
I cried
I hide
I mined my dreams And without working on that I lined my foolish failures…..

Will nimble my thoughts ,
Will accept my faults ,
Will grow more strong ,
Will prove my depressant side,
'You Messed With Wrong!'

Will climb the heights
Will shine in dark nights
This is to me and myself,
Though presently I am a looser….
But soon will smash them hard to hell's……

I know I am a silly storm inside….
And yes, I do have my own way to sparkle and ride….!

~ Anjali Shah

Gonna Grow Strong

There's Let no age bound to learn
Let yourself, get fall and burn
Let the people make your fun
You are gonna grow strong
You…are….gonna be right in those wrong

There's your way to shine
Let yourself be you and that's fine
Let the table turn at nine
You gonna grow strong
You….are…. gonna be right in those wrong

There's lots of loop holes
Let yourself be the free soul
Let the words enter your heart whole
You are gonna grow strong
You….are ….gonna be right in those wrong

~ *Anjali Shah*

11.
HIGHLY DIVINE ✨

Divine

Eyes that witnessed Love…
Their story is divine pleasure all of above…

" Radhe… Radhe…" was heard all around…
Flutes' melodious rhymes was ultimate sound…
Deep in love were their eyes,
With their story the world relieves…

Charming And Peaceful ,
Radha ' s Krishna the Naughtiest Divine ♡

~ *Anjali Shah*

Mickey And Minnie

Hands in hands,
And felt those vibes…
Some Small-Small talks,
And his heart hypes...

She was Minnie,
wearing pink short dress...
The red bow wearing, Mickey!
Got lost in her big eyelash ....

The couple was soon called Mr. & Mrs.
Cupid banged both of them in love fist ....!

~ *Anjali Shah*

12.
HEATH BEING PRIME

Yoga For Humanity

A bit by bit
And little by little
Let's touch the height
Being Calm and patience bright

Sages Wisdom
And Indians' Health Kingdom
Yoga being the Ultimate key
It's habit makes a human disease free

The world accepted
The culture is again respected
Yoga being shape of the life
Makes a person's soul alive

Gives You Serenity and Sanity
Yoga Is For Humanity.....

~ *Anjali Shah*

13
Over Dramatic

Hello To The Hell

Got a bad reputation
That's what I heard You saying
You need to you learn a lesson
I have more worth than you are playing

He said, 'Hello To The Hell'
Victim card, She plays that well
That's how he unfold the end

I really got a deep cut in
Oh gosh! Your love is still burning
I had So you my past trauma
So you called it all drama

All your All talks, Hypnotised
All my tears, Criticized
You treated me as if a goal
And so you kicked my I heart to score

He said, 'Hello To The Hell'
Victim card, She plays that well
That's how he unfold the end
You call yourself a player
One side game, that's how you win & lie layer

Still I would clap and cheer you up
You won you that bloody dating cup

I won't take a revenge back
Will answer you with I the class you lack
I have more worth than what you are playing
Hey, Look at me I am still slaying

He said, 'Hello To The Hell'
Victim card, She plays that well,
That's how he unfold the end

~ Anjali Shah

Dear Reader

I hope you enjoyed reading all the over dramatic titles and situations perception provided by the lively poetries….

I hope I get all your support to the work I did in this writing field….

If u liked it you can provide your feedback to below mentioned email id…

Email :- anjalishah5023@gmail.com

Hey Wait…. !

Can You Smile ?

😆*Yes your smile is precious….!*

And Don't Worry You Doing Good ♡

Salutation

I just want to thank my parents and my other closed ones who acknowledged me and brought confidence in me that I can portrait my thoughts the way I want….

And there's nothing wrong in that !

And yeah even thanks to the people who brought me great experiences and memories and absolutely content to write over …

Thank You